TAP and RAP, MOVE and GROOVE

Connie Bergstein Dow

Illustrated by Debbie Palen

free spirit
PUBLISHING®

DEDICATION

To my grandchildren, who love to move and groove: Ocean, Maggie, Emily, Elizabeth, Andrew, Logan, and the little one on the way

Text © 2024 Connie Bergstein Dow
Illustrations © 2024 Free Spirit Publishing

Free Spirit, Free Spirit Publishing, and associated logos are trademarks and/or registered trademarks of Teacher Created Materials. A complete listing of our logos and trademarks is available at freespirit.com

Library of Congress Cataloging-in-Publication Data
Names: Dow, Connie Bergstein, author. | Palen, Debbie, illustrator.
Title: Tap and rap, move and groove / Connie Bergstein Dow ; illustrated by Debbie Palen.
Description: Minneapolis, MN : Free Spirit Publishing, an imprint of
    Teacher Created Materials, Inc., 2024. | Audience: Ages 3–8
Identifiers: LCCN 2023004468 (print) | LCCN 2023004469 (ebook) | ISBN 9798885540520 (hardcover) | ISBN
    9798885540537 (ebook) | ISBN 9798885540544 (epub)
Subjects: LCSH: Dance—Juvenile literature. | BISAC: JUVENILE NONFICTION / Health & Daily Living / Fitness &
    Exercise | JUVENILE NONFICTION / Social Topics / Emotions & Feelings
Classification: LCC GV1596.5 .D68 2024 (print) | LCC GV1596.5 (ebook) | DDC 792.8—dc23/eng/20230310
LC record available at https://lccn.loc.gov/2023004468
LC ebook record available at https://lccn.loc.gov/2023004469

Edited by Marjorie Lisovskis
Cover and interior design by Colleen Pidel
Illustrated by Debbie Palen

Printed in China

Free Spirit Publishing
An imprint of Teacher Created Materials
9850 51st Avenue North, Suite 100
Minneapolis, MN 55442
(612) 338-2068
help4kids@freespirit.com
freespirit.com

FSC
www.fsc.org
MIX
Paper | Supporting responsible forestry
FSC® C144853

DANCE CHANTS

Lively FEET

Do your feet feel lively?
It's time for some fun!

Marching feet
keep a steady beat.

Twirling feet
like to turn and spin.

Tiptoeing feet
like to walk up high.

Hopping feet
like to bounce around.

Sneaking feet
are quiet as can be.

Sliding feet
like to slip and swirl.

Jumping feet
like to spring and leap.

Silly feet
have toes that wiggle.

Prancing feet
proudly point and strut.

Stomping feet
like to clomp and tromp.

Galloping feet
go *one-two-three, one-two-three.*

Tired feet
like to stop and rest . . .

Until they're ready
to start again!

ON YOUR Spot

Start on your spot.
Stand very tall.

Bounce on your spot.
March on your spot.

Sit on your spot.
Spin on your spot.

Stand back up—
Fast as you can.

Up on your tiptoes.
Turn around.

Jump on your spot.
Hop on your spot.

Balance on one foot.
Breathe and hold.

Balance on the other.
Breathe and hold.

Do a little dance.
Now freeze on your spot!

Melt on your spot,
Slowly, slowly.

Take a little rest,
Right on your spot.

Gallop Down the Line

Face your partner and take a bow.
Clap your hands and stomp your feet.
Join your hands and gallop down the line,
Take your place and wave to your friends!

WAVING RAP

Step and clap, step and clap,
As we do our waving rap!

Wave your head both up and down.
Show a smile and not a frown!

Step and clap, step and clap,
As we do our waving rap!

Wave your hands, way down low.
Wave your leg, and now your toes!

Step and clap, step and clap,
As we do our waving rap!

Wave your arms, way up high.
Reach your fingers to the sky.

Step and clap, step and clap,
As we do our waving rap!

Jump and hop, twist and bop.
Wave everything . . . and now we stop!

9

THUMBS UP

One thumb up. Other thumb up.
Tap your knees, then clap three times.

One thumb up. Other thumb up.
Reach up high on your tippy toes.

One thumb up. Other thumb up.
March around with your knees up high.

One thumb up. Other thumb up.
Balance on one foot as long as you can.

One thumb up. Other thumb up.
Stretch to the side, now the other side.

One thumb up. Other thumb up.
Do jumping jacks and count to four.

One thumb up. Other thumb up.
Sit right down, then stand again.

One thumb up. Other thumb up.
Run in place as fast as you can.

One thumb up. Other thumb up.
Move however you want to move.

Now it's time to end our dance.
Make a silly face with both thumbs up!

HAPPY, SAD, SHY, MAD, Silly

Make a happy face.
Take a happy pose.
When do you feel happy?
Do a happy dance.

Make a sad face.
Take a sad pose.
When do you feel sad?
Do a sad dance.

Make a shy face.
Take a shy pose.
When do you feel shy?
Do a shy dance.

Make a mad face.
Take a mad pose.
When do you feel mad?
Do a mad dance.

Make a silly face.
Take a silly pose.
When do you feel silly?
Do a silly dance!

QUACK, QUACK, QUACK, Moo!

Quack, quack, quack,
Mooooooooo!
Waddle like a duck
and moo like a cow.

Ruff, ruff, ruff,
Meooooooow!
Play like a dog
and meow like a cat.

Thump, thump, thump,
Whoooooooo!
Hop like a bunny
and hoot like an owl.

Grrrr, grrr, grrr,
Bzzzzzzzz!
Run like a bear
and buzz like a bee.

Swim, swim, swim.
Tweeeeeeeet!
Swim like a fish
and tweet like a bird.

Stomp, stomp. stomp,
Squeeeeeeak!
Stomp like an elephant
and squeak like a mouse.

MOOOO!

ONE, TWO, Cha-Cha-Cha

Let's start—here we go.
Step in place to the cha-cha beat!

Step, step, step-step-step.
One, two, cha-cha-cha.

Try it first, facing front.
One, two, cha-cha-cha.

Now turn to the side.
One, two, cha-cha-cha.

Turn back to the front.
One, two, cha-cha-cha.

Now turn the other way.
One, two, cha-cha-cha.

Come back to the front.
One, two, cha-cha-cha.

Travel forward, cha-cha-cha.
One, two, cha-cha-cha.

Forward again, cha-cha-cha.
One, two, cha-cha-cha.

Lift your arms, cha-cha-cha.
One, two, cha-cha-cha.

Say, "Woo-hoo!" cha-cha-cha.
One, two, cha-cha-cha.

Travel backward, cha-cha-cha.
One, two, cha-cha-cha.

Backward again, cha-cha-cha.
One, two, cha-cha-cha.

Let's go around the room.
One, two, cha-cha-cha.

Wave hello as you pass by.
One, two, cha-cha-cha.

Dance, dance, feel the beat.
One, two, cha-cha-cha.

One more time
and then we're done.
One, two, cha-cha-CHA!

FREEZE Dance

Do the grapevine to the side.
Do it again to the other side.
Stomp, clap, stomp, clap.
Freeze in a twisty, curly shape!

Do the grapevine to the side.
Do it again to the other side.
Stomp, clap, stomp, clap.
Freeze in a wide and stretchy shape!

Do the grapevine to the side.
Do it again to the other side.
Stomp, clap, stomp, clap.
Freeze in a very, very low shape!

Do the grapevine to the side.
Do it again to the other side.
Stomp, clap, stomp, clap.
Freeze in a sharp and pointy shape!

Do the grapevine to the side.
Do it again to the other side.
Stomp, clap, stomp, clap.
Freeze and balance on just one leg!

Do the grapevine to the side.
Do it again to the other side.
Stomp, clap, stomp, clap.
Freeze in a pose like you're feeling mad!

Do the grapevine to the side.
Do it again to the other side.
Stomp, clap, stomp, clap.
Freeze in a topsy-turvy shape!

Do the grapevine to the side.
Do it again to the other side.
Stomp, clap, stomp, clap.
Freeze in a pose on your tippy toes!

Do the grapevine to the side.
Do it again to the other side.
Stomp, clap, stomp, clap.
Freeze in your funniest silly shape!

TAPPITY Rap

Tap your toes, stomp three times.
This is how we tappity rap!

Stretch your arms out to the side.
High and low, high and low.

Tap your toes, stomp three times.
This is how we tappity rap!

Move your body in a happy wiggle-jiggle.
Squiggle and shimmy and shake, shake, shake.

Tap your toes, stomp three times.
This is how we tappity rap!

We're all done with our tappity rap.
Now let's take a great big bow!

Around the Circle

Sidestep once, then one more time.
Hands on your hips, and twist three times.
Jump in the circle and touch the floor.
Jump back out. What comes next?

Layla says we'll stomp our feet.
Stomp, stomp, stomp-stomp-stomp.

Cyrus says we'll touch our toes.
Reach and touch, reach and touch.

Joshua says we'll march and clap.
March and clap, march and clap.

Rosa says we'll turn around.
Turn around, turn around.

Amir says we'll tap our knees.
Tap, tap, tap-tap-tap.

Charlotte says we'll flap our wings.
Flap, flap, flap-flap-flap.

Now let's stop and end our dance.
Freeze!

HELLO, Astronauts!

Crouch down low and count with me.
10, 9, 8 . . .
7, 6, 5 . . .

All ready now, so here we go.
4, 3, 2, 1 . . .
Blast off!

Hold on tight as we soar into space.
Soar, soar,
Soar, soar.

We glide past planets and comets and stars.
Glide, glide,
Glide, glide.

Let's take a spacewalk—float and fly.
Float and fly,
Float and fly.

Out here in space we twist and spin.
Twist and spin,
Twist and spin.

Circle around and turn upside down.
Turn upside down,
Turn upside down.

Time to go home, let's return to the ship.
Fast as you can!
Fast as you can!

Can you steer us back to Earth?
Getting closer,
Getting closer.

Softly land.
Open the door.
People are cheering. Wave and bow.

Hello, astronauts—welcome home!

Conga Line

First let's clap the conga beat.
Quiet, quiet, quiet, **LOUD**.
Quiet, quiet, quiet, **LOUD**.

Try the rhythm in your feet.
Step, step, step, **STOMP**.
Step, step, step, **STOMP**.

Try it walking, follow me.
Step, step, step, **STOMP**.
Step, step, step, **STOMP**.

Move along in our conga line.
Step, step, step, **STOMP**.
Step, step, step, **STOMP**.

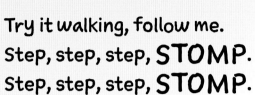

Conga line goes all around.
Step, step, step, STOMP.
Step, step, step, STOMP.

Wave your hand out to the side.
Step, step, step, STOMP.
Step, step, step, STOMP.

Now wave to the other side.
Step, step, step, STOMP.
Step, step, step, STOMP.

Conga dance is almost done.
Step, step, step, STOMP.
Step . . . step . . . step . . . STOP!

Earth DANCE

Roosters crowing
Sunrise glowing

Pups prancing
Sunlight dancing

Geese gliding
Clouds sliding

Doves cooing
Storm brewing

Tigers leaping
Winds sweeping

Whales slapping
Thunder clapping

Cheetahs dashing
Lightning flashing

Frogs hopping
Raindrops plopping

Penguins marching
Rainbow arching

Moths swirling
Mist curling

Birds nesting
Babies resting

Owls calling
Shadows falling

Insects humming
Night coming

Eyes closing
Animals dozing

Moon gleaming
Children dreaming

Leading Creative Dance Chants WITH YOUNG CHILDREN

Following are a few simple steps that will make it easy to introduce and lead dance chants with young children.

The Basics

1. **Select a chant.** Read the chant to yourself and review the guidelines on the next pages for the chant you have chosen.

2. **Read the chant aloud to children,** just as you would a new poem or story. Say each line, and ask children to repeat it.

3. **Explain the basic structure.** For example, say, "We're going to do an activity called 'On Your Spot.' We'll each stand in one place and discover many ways we can move on one spot. I will say the words, and you can try the movements." If the chant is one that children will say along with you, such as "Tappity Rap," repeat the words with them several times before adding movements.

4. **Add the movements that go with the words.** Try the activity slowly, then increase the speed as you and the children become more comfortable performing the words and movements together.

5. **Repeat whenever you wish.** The digital content (go.freespirit. com/2dance) offers ideas to vary, expand, and add music to the activities. Consider performing a favorite dance chant informally for friends and family.

Tips for Smooth Dancing

Young children will gain the most benefit from movement activities when you establish clear boundaries. The following guidelines will help you lead each dance chant activity smoothly from start to finish.

Spatial parameters. Dance activities can take place in virtually any space. Large, unobstructed spaces (such as a gym, classroom, or outdoor area) work well for up to 10 children. If there are more, arrange them in smaller groups. Many of the chants can be done in small or partially obstructed spaces. If the movement stays on or near a home spot, each child can perform the chant in a small area.

Cues. For any dance activity, designate a cue that signals *stop*, so that you can immediately regain the group's attention. Auditory cues include a tambourine, drum, short song, or rhythmic clapping. For visual cues, you might flick the lights, show a stop sign, or use a hand signal. After pausing, review the instructions and then resume the activity.

Home spots. At the beginning of every chant, assign a home spot for each child. Home spots might be vinyl dots, tape, or mats. Any time you need to rein in the energy, ask everyone to return to their home spots.

Traffic flow. To help children learn to move together in a large space, guide them to move in a specific direction. For example, during "Lively Feet," have children go from their starting places toward the front of the room for the first prompt, marching. For the next prompt, twirling, ask them to cross the room in the other direction or move in a circle. Use this approach for all chants when children are moving freely together.

Pauses. Make sure to pause when the chant offers a movement prompt. During pauses, give children an opportunity to explore the prompt through movement. Once they have tried various actions, continue on.

Alternating groups. When you have more than 10 children and need to alternate them in dancing, it can be an opportunity for learning. Children will practice impulse control as they wait. They'll watch the ways other children move, which might inspire new ideas. It is also an opportunity to learn to be a respectful audience member.

A quiet finish. Most of the dance chant activities include a way to bring children's energy down to a quiet conclusion, to prepare everyone to transition to the next part of the day.

Incorporating music. The chants are designed to be used as their own accompaniment, with the words spoken while dancing. However, music and dance are natural partners, and music, drumming, or clapping a beat can all enhance the chants. Download the digital content about music to use.

Guidelines for Leading Each Chant

Lively Feet (page 2). With everyone starting in home spots spread throughout the space, chant the first stanza and ask children to repeat it. Then allow them to respond to the words, moving together in a specific direction, such as across the space or around in a circle. Pause; repeat for each stanza.

On Your Spot (page 4). Children start and remain on home spots spread throughout the space. Chant in a 1-2 beat, pausing after each line for children to move.

Gallop Down the Line (page 6). Children stand side by side in two lines facing each other, a few feet apart. Chant the words together and clap as the first two children at the head of each line dance the movements and then gallop together down the center, taking their places at the ends of the lines. The next pair of children do the same. Continue until all children have had turns.

Waving Rap (page 8). Children perform the chant and movements while staying close to their starting places, standing either on home spots or in staggered lines of 4 or 5 children, facing front. For each "Step and clap" stanza, children step to one side while clapping, then to the other side, and then wave both hands.

Thumbs Up (page 10). Children stand in pairs facing each other or in groups in a loose circle. Chant and dance the first line of each stanza together with children. Call out the prompt in the second line, and have children respond with movement.

Happy, Sad, Shy, Mad, Silly (page 12). Say the words of each stanza slowly, giving children time to respond to each line. Each child stays close to their home spot while responding to the prompts. Allow a longer pause after the last line of every stanza.

Quack, Quack, Quack, Moo! (page 14). Say the full chant aloud. Then say the first two lines of the first stanza, and ask children to chant them back to you. Say the third and fourth lines, and invite children to respond with movement and sound. Repeat with each stanza.

One, Two, Cha-Cha-Cha! (page 16). Everyone stands in a circle, arm's length apart. Chant the introductory stanza. Then call out the first line of each following stanza, with everyone chanting "One, two, cha-cha-cha!" as they dance. Children are not meant to move quickly, so they can easily navigate around each other.

Freeze Dance (page 18). Everyone says the first three lines of each stanza together while dancing. Call out the last line of the stanza and have children freeze in different shapes.

Tappity Rap (page 20). Children stay close to their home spots and perform the chant and movements together. Start in staggered lines of 4 or 5 children per line, facing front. For the "Tap your toes" stanza, tap the toes of one foot twice, then stomp feet three times. Wave hands in front, palms out, for the second line.

Around the Circle (page 22). Everyone stands in a circle, arm's length apart. Chant in a 1-2-3-4 beat and do the movements together. Designed to be expanded, the activity prompts each child to contribute an idea as you build the dance together. Each time you perform it, do the first four-line stanza, then each of the new stanzas, always in the same order.

Hello, Astronauts! (page 24). For this imaginary trip to outer space, call out the words, pausing after each line for children to try different movement ideas.

Conga Line (page 26). Everyone lines up behind a leader for this dance. Start leading and saying the words as everyone dances. Once children are familiar with the words and steps, they can take turns being the leader. In an open space, the leader can move freely. In an obstructed space, they can lead the line around tables, chairs, and other obstacles.

Earth Dance (page 28). In this dance, children move freely throughout the available space. Chant the first stanza and ask children to repeat it. Then encourage children to respond to the words, moving together in a specific direction, such as across the space or around in a circle. Repeat for each stanza. When you reach the phrase "Birds nesting," begin to chant softly and slowly; for "Shadows falling," prompt children to slowly drop to the ground, close their eyes, and listen quietly to the final verses.

The Benefits of Creative Dance for Young Children

Dance chants open the door to a world of imaginative movement and literacy experiences for young children; they also offer opportunities for social-emotional skill development.

Physical development. Dance helps children develop both large- and fine-motor skills, coordination, flexibility, balance, and strength. Like other forms of exercise, it can improve cardiovascular health.

Early literacy. In the dance chant format, children use movement and spoken words together. This process can help them develop new vocabulary, recognize rhythm, and practice multitasking skills.

Creativity. The art form of dance stimulates creativity and imagination. Open-ended problem-solving prompts that are inherent in dance chants allow children to use new approaches in their search for solutions through movement.

Social-emotional skill development. Dance offers the perfect arena for nurturing social-emotional learning skills, providing a variety of ways for children to interact. As they explore personal and shared space, children work on developing relationship skills and practice goal-directed behavior, decision-making, personal responsibility, impulse control, self-management, and a host of other essential skills.

MAKING DANCE CHANTS ACCESSIBLE

Most dance activities can be adapted and modified for various learners and needs. The following examples suggest ways to include everyone and may spark other ideas for you as well.

- Divide the chants into smaller segments. Teach a single line or stanza, along with the corresponding movement, before moving on.

- Use cues that are visual, auditory, or a combination of both.

- Delineate spatial boundaries with objects, such as cones or taped lines.

- For children with sensory sensitivities, eliminate any accompaniment. Dimming the lights and shortening the activity's duration may also be helpful.

- Invite a child to chant along with you. You can quietly prompt them with the upcoming line, and they can then call it out.

- Ask a child to help you keep the beat with a small percussion instrument.

- Have a child participate by assisting you with the visual and auditory cues.

- Modify the words: "Tap your toes" can become "Tap your hands," "Blink your eyes," or "Nod your head." "Do the grapevine to the side" can become "Stretch your arms out to the side."

- In any chant where the response is open-ended and children are prompted to move freely, a child with a mobility condition can move however they are willing and able.

ABOUT THE AUTHOR AND ILLUSTRATOR

Author and dance educator Connie Bergstein Dow graduated from Denison University and has an MFA from the University of Michigan. She has danced professionally in the United States, Venezuela, and Guatemala, and has taught dance to all ages, from toddlers to senior adults. Connie shares her passion for movement by writing picture books (including *From A to Z with Energy!*), verses, articles, and books for teachers about integrating dance into the curriculum. She loves connecting with young readers at schools and libraries and conducting movement workshops for early childhood professionals. Connie divides her time between Cincinnati, Ohio, and Boulder, Colorado.
Find her at movingislearning.com.

Debbie Palen is a professional illustrator in children's publishing. Her work has been recognized by the Educational Press Association, *Print* magazine, *How* magazine, *Highlights for Children*, and the 2020 Northern Lights Award in middle grade fiction. When not illustrating, she can be found walking in the woods, doing yoga, writing, reading kids' books, dancing to many different kinds of music, or eating dark chocolate. Debbie lives in Cleveland, Ohio, with one human and one very fuzzy animal that might be a cat.